Operation Valkyrie: The Key Individuals Behind Hitler's Assassination Attempt

Copyright Page

TITLE: Operation Valkyrie: The Key Individuals Behind Hitler's Assassination Attempt

1ST Edition

Copyright @ 2023

ISBN: 9798223840749

Table of Contents

Operation Valkyrie: The Key Individuals Behind Hitler's Assassination Attempt

By Roberto Miguel Rodriguez

Chapter 1: Operation Valkyrie: The Failed Assassination Attempt Against Adolf Hitler

Historical Context: Germany in the mid-1940s

In order to fully understand the significance of Operation Valkyrie, it is essential to examine the historical context in which it took place. Germany in the mid-1940s was a nation deeply entrenched in the horrors of World War II and the oppressive regime of Adolf Hitler.

At this point in the war, Germany had already conquered much of Europe and established a brutal occupation in the territories under its control. Hitler's Nazi regime had implemented a series of racist and discriminatory policies, targeting Jews, Romani people, disabled individuals, and other marginalized groups for extermination. The German war machine was in full swing, with the Holocaust in motion and the German army fighting on multiple fronts.

Within Germany, resistance to Hitler's regime was present, but it was fragmented and faced immense challenges. The Gestapo, Hitler's secret police, were ruthless in their pursuit of dissenters, and anyone suspected of opposing the regime faced imprisonment, torture, or execution. Despite these risks, a number of individuals within Germany's military, intelligence, and civilian sectors became disillusioned with Hitler's leadership and sought to take action.

Operation Valkyrie was born out of this resistance movement, led by Colonel Claus von Stauffenberg and a group of like-minded individuals who believed that assassinating Hitler was the only way to save Germany from further destruction. Their plan was to use the existing military infrastructure to seize control of the government and negotiate a peace treaty with the Allies, effectively ending the war.

However, the conspirators faced numerous obstacles. The Nazi regime had established a vast intelligence network and had spies within its own ranks. The intricate planning required to carry out the assassination plot was fraught with challenges, and the conspirators had to carefully navigate the power struggles and internal conflicts within the Nazi party.

Furthermore, the failed assassination attempt had far-reaching consequences. Hitler's survival led to a brutal crackdown on the resistance movement, resulting in the execution of thousands of individuals suspected of involvement. The failed plot also solidified Hitler's grip on power and further radicalized his regime.

The mid-1940s in Germany were a time of desperation and uncertainty. Operation Valkyrie emerged as a beacon of hope for those who believed that Hitler's rule could be brought to an end. Despite its ultimate failure, the assassination attempt and the individuals involved in it serve as a testament to the courage and determination of those who risked everything to oppose Hitler's regime. Understanding the historical context of Germany in the mid-1940s allows us to fully appreciate the significance of Operation Valkyrie and its lasting impact on history.

The Rise of Adolf Hitler and the Nazi Party

The rise of Adolf Hitler and the Nazi Party is a pivotal chapter in the history of the world, and particularly in the context of Operation Valkyrie. To truly understand the failed assassination attempt against Hitler, it is crucial to delve into the events and circumstances that led to his ascension to power.

Adolf Hitler, a charismatic and persuasive speaker, used the disillusionment and economic turmoil following World War I to his advantage. He capitalized on the German people's deep-seated resentment towards the Treaty of Versailles, which imposed severe reparations and territorial losses on Germany. Hitler's promises of restoring German pride and reclaiming lost territories struck a chord with the struggling populace.

The Nazi Party, under Hitler's leadership, quickly gained popularity and support. Their propaganda machine, led by Joseph Goebbels, skillfully manipulated public opinion and exploited the fears and prejudices of the German population. Hitler's message of Aryan supremacy and the scapegoating of minority groups resonated with many, leading to a surge in Nazi party membership.

As Hitler consolidated his power, he implemented a series of policies that systematically dismantled the democratic institutions of the Weimar Republic. The Enabling Act of 1933 effectively granted Hitler dictatorial powers, allowing him to bypass the Reichstag and rule by decree. The Nazi regime then embarked on a campaign of persecution against political opponents, minority groups, and anyone deemed a threat to the regime.

The internal conflicts within the Nazi party also played a significant role in the events leading up to Operation Valkyrie. Several high-ranking officials, including those involved in the assassination plot, were disillusioned with Hitler's leadership and the direction of the regime. These individuals, motivated by a sense of duty and a desire to save Germany from further destruction, saw the assassination of Hitler as the only solution.

The rise of Hitler and the Nazi Party set the stage for Operation Valkyrie. The failed assassination attempt was not only a reflection of the internal conflicts within Nazi Germany but also a testament to the courage and determination of those who risked their lives to oppose Hitler's regime.

In the following subchapters, we will explore the historical context, the motivations of the key individuals involved in the assassination plot, the intricacies of the failed operation, and the subsequent impact on

Hitler's rule and the course of the war. We will also delve into the various conspiracy theories surrounding Operation Valkyrie and the cultural influence of this extraordinary event. By examining these aspects, we can gain a deeper understanding of the complexities of political assassinations in history and the motivations that drive individuals to take such extreme measures.

Overview of Operation Valkyrie: Objectives and Execution

Operation Valkyrie, also known as the 1944 failed assassination attempt against Adolf Hitler, remains a significant event in history, captivating the attention of historians and enthusiasts alike. This subchapter aims to provide a comprehensive overview of the operation, shedding light on its objectives and execution.

At its core, Operation Valkyrie sought to eliminate Adolf Hitler and dismantle the Nazi regime in Germany. The key individuals involved in this audacious plot were driven by a shared belief that Hitler's leadership was detrimental to the nation and that his removal would pave the way for a new Germany. This included high-ranking military officers, politicians, and members of the German resistance movements.

The execution of Operation Valkyrie was meticulously planned and involved a multi-faceted approach. The conspirators intended to assassinate Hitler during a meeting at the Wolf's Lair, his heavily fortified headquarters. Colonel Claus von Stauffenberg, a key figure in the operation, was responsible for planting a bomb in a briefcase near Hitler during the meeting. However, due to a series of unfortunate events, the bomb only managed to wound Hitler, allowing him to survive.

The aftermath of the failed assassination attempt led to a flurry of military actions and internal conflicts within Nazi Germany. Hitler's survival triggered a brutal crackdown on the conspirators and resistance movements, resulting in arrests, trials, and executions. The operation's failure also had significant implications for the course of World War II, as Hitler's survival allowed him to continue leading the Nazi war effort.

Operation Valkyrie and its key individuals have since become subjects of intrigue and fascination, inspiring numerous conspiracy theories and studies on military strategy and tactics. Historians have delved into the motivations and mindset of the conspirators, analyzing their psychological profiles to better understand their actions.

Furthermore, the story of Operation Valkyrie has had a profound cultural influence, being depicted in various forms of popular culture. Literature, film, and other mediums have explored the event, offering different perspectives and interpretations of the failed assassination attempt.

In conclusion, Operation Valkyrie represents a pivotal moment in history, showcasing the bravery and determination of those who dared to oppose Hitler's regime. This subchapter serves as an introduction to the objectives and execution of the operation, providing a foundation for deeper exploration into the various niches surrounding Operation Valkyrie.

Chapter 2: Key Individuals Behind the Assassination Attempt

Claus von Stauffenberg: The Mastermind of Operation Valkyrie

Claus von Stauffenberg, a German army officer, is widely recognized as the mastermind behind Operation Valkyrie, the daring and audacious assassination attempt against Adolf Hitler during World War II. This subchapter delves into the fascinating life and background of Stauffenberg, shedding light on his motivations, mindset, and the intricate planning that went into the failed plot.

Born in 1907 into a noble family, Stauffenberg grew up in a conservative environment shaped by traditional values and a deep sense of duty. His military career began in the 1930s, where he quickly rose through the ranks, displaying exceptional leadership skills and a keen understanding of military strategy. However, it was his growing disillusionment with Hitler's regime and its atrocities that eventually led him to become a key figure in the German resistance movement.

Stauffenberg's involvement in Operation Valkyrie was fueled by a desire to rid Germany of Hitler's tyrannical rule and to restore honor and integrity to the country. Recognizing the need for a decisive blow against the Nazi regime, Stauffenberg meticulously devised a plan to assassinate Hitler and seize control of the government.

The subchapter explores the intricate details of Stauffenberg's plan, highlighting the challenges he faced, such as infiltrating Hitler's inner circle and coordinating the actions of his fellow conspirators. It also examines the military strategy and tactics employed during the failed assassination attempt and the subsequent military actions that unfolded.

Furthermore, this subchapter delves into the various resistance movements and individuals within Germany who opposed Hitler's regime. It sheds light on the power struggles and internal conflicts within the Nazi party that fueled the assassination attempt, as well as the intelligence networks and secret operations involved in planning the operation.

Moreover, the subchapter analyzes the consequences and aftermath of the failed assassination attempt on Hitler's rule and the course of the war. It also delves into the cultural influence of Operation Valkyrie, exploring how the story has been depicted in literature, film, and other forms of popular culture.

Lastly, the subchapter provides a psychological profile of Stauffenberg and the other conspirators, delving into their motivations and mindset. It examines the ethical dilemmas they faced, their sense of duty, and the risks they were willing to take to bring about change.

In conclusion, this subchapter offers historians and enthusiasts of Operation Valkyrie a comprehensive exploration of Claus von Stauffenberg, the mastermind behind the audacious assassination attempt against Hitler. It provides valuable insights into his life, motivations, and the intricacies of the failed plot, shedding light on the broader historical context, military strategy, and the German resistance movements during World War II.

Henning von Tresckow: The Strategist and Co-Conspirator

Henning von Tresckow, a key figure in Operation Valkyrie, was a remarkable strategist and co-conspirator who played a critical role in the failed assassination attempt against Adolf Hitler in 1944. As a historian, it is essential to delve into the life and background of this enigmatic individual to understand the intricacies of the plot and its significance in World War II history.

Born into a noble Prussian family, von Tresckow was deeply rooted in German military tradition. His experiences during World War I shaped his perspective, leaving him disillusioned with the increasingly totalitarian Nazi regime in which he found himself during World War II. Recognizing the danger Hitler posed to Europe and humanity, von Tresckow became a key figure in the German resistance movement.

Von Tresckow's remarkable military mind allowed him to strategize and plan Operation Valkyrie meticulously. Understanding the importance of removing Hitler from power, he sought to orchestrate an assassination that would pave the way for a coup and bring an end to the Nazi regime. His ability to navigate the complex web of conspirators, politicians, and military officials was instrumental in bringing together various factions of the resistance movement.

This subchapter will delve into von Tresckow's motivations and the mindset that drove him to risk everything to rid Germany of Hitler's oppressive rule. By examining his background, we gain insights into his determination, courage, and unwavering belief in the righteousness of the cause.

Moreover, it is crucial to analyze von Tresckow's strategic brilliance and the military tactics employed during Operation Valkyrie. By dissecting the failed assassination plot and the subsequent military actions, historians can gain a deeper understanding of the challenges faced by the conspirators and the impact their actions had on the course of the war.

Furthermore, exploring von Tresckow's role within the broader resistance movement and the internal conflicts within Nazi Germany sheds light on the power struggles and ideological clashes that fueled the assassination attempt. This subchapter will investigate the various resistance groups and individuals who opposed Hitler's regime, highlighting the significance of von Tresckow's contributions within this larger context.

Lastly, the subchapter will examine the consequences and aftermath of Operation Valkyrie on Hitler's rule and the course of the war. By analyzing the impacts of the failed assassination attempt, historians can evaluate the long-term effects on the German resistance movement, the Nazi regime, and the war itself.

Henning von Tresckow's story is not only a testament to his character but also a case study in political assassinations and the complexities of resistance movements during wartime. By exploring his life, motivations, and strategic brilliance, historians can gain a deeper understanding of Operation Valkyrie and its significance in World War II history.

Ludwig Beck: The Military Leader and Opponent of Hitler

Ludwig Beck, a highly decorated military leader and key figure in the German resistance movement, was one of the key individuals involved in the failed assassination attempt against Adolf Hitler known as Operation Valkyrie. As a renowned military strategist and tactician, Beck played a crucial role in the planning and execution of the plot, which aimed to overthrow Hitler's regime and bring an end to the atrocities committed by the Nazi regime during World War II.

Born in 1880, Beck rose through the ranks of the German military, eventually becoming the Chief of the General Staff of the Army in 1935. However, despite his high-ranking position, Beck became increasingly disillusioned with Hitler's leadership and his aggressive policies that were leading Germany towards war. Recognizing the danger Hitler posed to Germany and the world, Beck joined forces with other like-minded individuals within the German military and civilian sectors to plan the assassination of Hitler.

Beck's involvement in Operation Valkyrie was driven by his unwavering belief that Hitler's removal from power was necessary to save Germany from further destruction and restore its reputation in the international community. He believed that the assassination would trigger a coup against the Nazi regime and pave the way for a peaceful resolution to the war. However, the attempt on Hitler's life failed on July 20, 1944, leading to severe consequences for Beck and the other conspirators.

Following the failed assassination attempt, Beck was implicated in the plot and faced the choice between surrendering to the Gestapo or taking his own life. In a final act of defiance against Hitler's tyranny, Beck chose to commit suicide, becoming a martyr for the German resistance movement.

Beck's actions and his role in Operation Valkyrie had a profound impact on the course of World War II and the German resistance movement. His unwavering commitment to his principles and his willingness to risk everything for the greater good make him a symbol of courage and integrity.

Today, historians continue to study and analyze the life and motivations of Ludwig Beck, seeking to understand the complex dynamics that led to the failed assassination attempt against Hitler. Through their research, they shed light on the significance of Operation Valkyrie in the context of German resistance movements, military strategy and tactics, and the broader history of political assassinations. Ludwig Beck's legacy serves as a reminder of the power of conviction and the willingness of individuals to stand up against tyranny, even in the face of insurmountable odds.

Other Notable Conspirators: Profiles and Roles in the Plot

In this subchapter, we delve into the lives and backgrounds of the other notable conspirators involved in Operation Valkyrie, the failed assassination attempt against Adolf Hitler in 1944. These individuals played crucial roles in the plot, each bringing their unique skills and motivations to the table.

One such conspirator is General Ludwig Beck, a key figure in the German resistance movement. As a former Chief of the Army General Staff, Beck held extensive military knowledge and strategic insights. His opposition to Hitler's leadership and his desire to restore Germany's reputation as a respected nation drove him to join the plot.

Another important figure was Colonel Claus von Stauffenberg, the mastermind behind the assassination attempt. Known for his unwavering commitment to the cause, von Stauffenberg was a highly decorated officer who believed it was his duty to end Hitler's reign of terror. His expertise in military tactics and access to high-ranking officials made him an invaluable asset to the conspiracy.

Count Helmuth James von Moltke, a lawyer and member of the German nobility, brought his legal expertise and connections to the resistance movement. He played a crucial role in coordinating the efforts of various resistance groups and ensuring their actions were aligned with the overall plan.

Other notable conspirators included General Friedrich Olbricht, who facilitated the military logistics of the plot, and Colonel Albrecht Mertz von Quirnheim, who helped coordinate the coup attempt from within the army. Their dedication to the cause and their strategic acumen were instrumental in the planning and execution of Operation Valkyrie.

While each conspirator had their own motivations and unique skills, they all shared a common goal: to rid Germany of Hitler's oppressive regime. Their collaboration and unwavering determination to carry out the assassination plot showcased the strength of the German resistance movement and their commitment to creating a better future for their country.

Their stories not only shed light on the individuals behind the assassination attempt, but also provide insights into the broader context of World War II, the internal conflicts within Nazi Germany, and the power struggles that shaped the course of history.

By examining the profiles and roles of these notable conspirators, we gain a deeper understanding of the complexities surrounding Operation Valkyrie and the countless acts of courage and sacrifice that went into challenging Hitler's rule. Their stories serve as a testament to the indomitable spirit of those who dared to resist, even in the face of seemingly insurmountable odds.

Chapter 3: World War II Conspiracies: Theories Surrounding Operation Valkyrie and Hitler's Survival

The Myth of Hitler's Escape

One of the most enduring conspiracy theories surrounding World War II and Operation Valkyrie is the belief that Adolf Hitler managed to escape and survive the war. Despite overwhelming evidence to the contrary, this myth continues to captivate the imaginations of many. However, a closer examination of the facts reveals that Hitler's escape is nothing more than a product of fiction and speculation.

First and foremost, it is important to note that Hitler's body was discovered by Soviet troops in his bunker in Berlin on April 30, 1945. His remains were later positively identified through dental records and other means of forensic analysis. The extensive documentation and eyewitness testimonies surrounding Hitler's death leave no room for doubt regarding his demise.

Furthermore, the notion that Hitler could have successfully evaded capture and lived out his days in hiding is highly implausible. The Allied forces were relentless in their pursuit of Nazi war criminals, and Hitler, as the leader of the Third Reich, would have been their primary target. The idea that he could have slipped away unnoticed and established a new life elsewhere is simply not feasible.

In addition to the lack of evidence supporting Hitler's escape, there is a wealth of evidence contradicting such claims. The accounts of those who were present in the bunker during Hitler's final days, such as his secretary Traudl Junge and his adjutant Otto Günsche, provide detailed descriptions of his deteriorating physical and mental state. These firsthand testimonies paint a vivid picture of a man on the brink of defeat and despair, far from someone plotting a daring escape.

The myth of Hitler's escape can be attributed, in part, to the psychological need for closure and the desire to find a glimmer of hope amidst the horrors of war. However, it is crucial for historians to rely on factual evidence and critical analysis when examining historical events. The overwhelming evidence points to Hitler's demise in the bunker, and it is through a rigorous examination of these facts that we can separate historical truth from myth.

In conclusion, the belief in Hitler's escape is a myth that persists in popular culture and conspiracy circles. However, a careful examination of the evidence reveals that it is nothing more than speculation and fiction. By dispelling this myth, we can focus on the true significance of Operation Valkyrie and the individuals involved in the failed assassination attempt against Hitler, shedding light on their motivations, strategies, and the broader historical context in which they operated.

Conspiracy Theories: Did the Assassination Attempt Succeed?

The failed assassination attempt against Adolf Hitler in 1944, known as Operation Valkyrie, has been the subject of numerous conspiracy theories. While historical records indicate that the plot did not ultimately succeed, some theorists speculate otherwise, suggesting that Hitler may have survived the attack. This subchapter delves into these conspiracy theories and explores the evidence surrounding Hitler's alleged survival.

One of the most persistent theories is that Hitler used a body double to deceive the conspirators and escape unharmed. Supporters of this theory point to discrepancies in eyewitness testimonies and the lack of conclusive evidence confirming Hitler's death. They argue that the body found in the bunker was not Hitler's, but rather that of his body double.

They suggest that Hitler may have fled to a secret location, where he lived out the remainder of his life.

Another theory proposes that high-ranking Nazi officials staged Hitler's death to divert attention and facilitate their own escape. This theory suggests that the assassination attempt was part of a larger plan to dismantle the Nazi regime from within. Proponents argue that Hitler's alleged survival would explain the subsequent chaos within the Nazi leadership and the disarray of the German military.

While these conspiracy theories may seem intriguing, historians largely dismiss them as far-fetched and lacking in credible evidence. The overwhelming consensus is that Hitler did not survive the assassination attempt, and his remains were indeed found in the bunker. Extensive documentation, including eyewitness accounts, corroborates this conclusion.

However, the existence of conspiracy theories surrounding Operation Valkyrie highlights the enduring fascination with Hitler's regime and the desire to uncover hidden truths. These theories also shed light on the psychological impact of Hitler's rule and the desperate measures some individuals were willing to take to bring about his downfall.

In conclusion, the conspiracy theories surrounding the success of the assassination attempt against Adolf Hitler in Operation Valkyrie have captivated imaginations for decades. While these theories may offer a tantalizing glimpse into the possibility of Hitler's survival, the weight of historical evidence supports the view that the attempt ultimately failed. Nonetheless, the enduring interest in this topic serves as a reminder of the complex motivations and actions of those involved in the plot, as well as the lasting impact of Hitler's rule on the world.

Examination of Alleged Sightings and Claims of Hitler's Survival

One of the most enduring and controversial aspects of Operation Valkyrie and the failed assassination attempt against Adolf Hitler is the question of his survival. In the aftermath of the plot, numerous claims and alleged sightings of Hitler emerged, leading to intense speculation and conspiracy theories that he had somehow managed to escape and evade capture.

Historians have delved into these claims, meticulously examining the evidence and testimonies put forth by those who claimed to have encountered Hitler after the events of July 20, 1944. The aim is to separate fact from fiction and shed light on the truth behind these alleged sightings.

Several individuals, such as former members of Hitler's inner circle, reported seeing him alive in the days and weeks following the assassination attempt. These testimonies, often conflicting and unreliable, have been carefully scrutinized by historians seeking to establish their veracity. In some cases, it became apparent that these sightings were either fabricated or mistaken identities, fueled by the chaos and confusion that gripped Germany during that tumultuous time.

Furthermore, the examination of alleged sightings also extends to the claims of Hitler's survival in distant locations such as South America. Reports of Hitler living out his days in Argentina or Brazil gained traction in the post-war years, with purported evidence ranging from eyewitness testimonies to alleged photographic proof. Historians have thoroughly investigated these claims, analyzing the available evidence and cross-referencing it with historical records and testimonies from those involved in the search for Hitler.

Ultimately, the overwhelming consensus among historians is that Adolf Hitler died by suicide in his bunker in Berlin on April 30, 1945. The extensive research and investigation into the alleged sightings and claims of his survival have failed to produce any conclusive evidence to the contrary.

However, the examination of these alleged sightings and claims is crucial in understanding the impact and influence of Operation Valkyrie. It reveals the enduring fascination with Hitler's fate and the lengths to which conspiracy theories can capture the public imagination. By exploring these claims, historians gain insight into the broader cultural and psychological implications of the failed assassination attempt and its aftermath.

In conclusion, the examination of alleged sightings and claims of Hitler's survival is a vital aspect of the historical analysis surrounding Operation Valkyrie. Through a meticulous and critical examination of the evidence, historians have sought to establish the truth behind these claims and shed light on the enduring mysteries surrounding Adolf Hitler's fate.

Chapter 4: Military Strategy and Tactics: The Intricacies of the Failed Assassination Plot

Planning and Execution of Operation Valkyrie

Operation Valkyrie: The Untold Stories of the Key Individuals Behind the Assassination Attempt

Chapter Subtitle: Planning and Execution of Operation Valkyrie

Introduction:

Operation Valkyrie, the 1944 failed assassination attempt against Adolf Hitler, remains one of the most captivating events in World War II history. This subchapter delves into the intricate planning and execution of the operation, shedding light on the key individuals involved and the strategies employed in their audacious plot.

I. The Conspirators and Their Motivations:

The meticulous planning of Operation Valkyrie relied on a diverse group of individuals driven by a shared desire to rid Germany of Hitler and end the atrocities of the Nazi regime. This section explores the backgrounds, motivations, and psychological profiles of the conspirators, offering insights into their decision to risk their lives for the greater good.

II. Intelligence Networks and Secret Operations:

To successfully execute Operation Valkyrie, the conspirators had to navigate the treacherous world of intelligence and espionage during World War II. This section delves into the intricate web of secret operations, covert communications, and intelligence networks involved in the planning process, highlighting the conspirators' resourcefulness and determination.

III. Military Strategy and Tactics:

Operation Valkyrie required careful consideration of military strategy and tactics. This section analyzes the intricacies of the failed assassination plot, including the selection of the Wolf's Lair as the location for the attempt, the timing of the explosion, and the contingency plans for seizing control of the government. It also explores the subsequent military actions during the war that shaped the outcome of the operation.

IV. Nazi Germany's Internal Conflicts:

Behind the scenes of Operation Valkyrie lay a web of power struggles and internal conflicts within the Nazi party. This section examines the factors that led to the assassination attempt, including the growing disillusionment with Hitler's leadership and the desire to save Germany from further destruction.

V. Impacts and Aftermath:

The consequences of Operation Valkyrie were far-reaching, both for Hitler's rule and the course of the war. This section examines the immediate aftermath, including the swift retribution faced by the conspirators and the implications for the German resistance movement. It also explores the long-term impact of the failed assassination attempt on the outcome of World War II.

Conclusion:

Operation Valkyrie stands as a testament to the bravery and determination of those who dared to oppose Hitler's regime. This subchapter provides a comprehensive exploration of the planning and execution of the operation, offering historians and enthusiasts a deeper understanding of the key individuals, military strategies, and political dynamics that shaped this pivotal moment in history.

The Bombing at the Wolf's Lair: How the Plan Went Awry

In the subchapter "The Bombing at the Wolf's Lair: How the Plan Went Awry," we delve deep into the intricacies of Operation Valkyrie, one of the most audacious assassination attempts against Adolf Hitler during World War II. This subchapter focuses on the key individuals involved in the plot, their motivations, and the unexpected turn of events that led to the plan's failure.

The Wolf's Lair, Hitler's heavily fortified headquarters, seemed like the perfect target for the conspirators. Led by Colonel Claus von Stauffenberg, a high-ranking officer within the German military, the plan was to plant a bomb inside Hitler's conference room during a meeting. The explosion would eliminate Hitler and trigger a coup d'état, which would overthrow the Nazi regime and end the war.

However, as history has shown, the plan did not go as intended. On July 20, 1944, von Stauffenberg successfully planted the bomb but was forced to leave the room before it detonated. The blast destroyed much of the conference room, but Hitler survived with only minor injuries.

In this subchapter, we explore the factors that contributed to the failure of the assassination attempt. We analyze the meticulous planning that went into the operation, including the selection of the Wolf's Lair as the target and the intricate network of conspirators involved. We also examine the flaws in execution that ultimately led to the plan's unraveling.

Moreover, we delve into the immediate aftermath of the bombing and the consequences it had on Germany, the war, and the individuals involved. We investigate the swift retaliation by the Nazi regime, which resulted in the capture, torture, and execution of many of the conspirators.

To understand the full context of the failed assassination attempt, we also explore the internal conflicts within Nazi Germany that fueled the resistance movement. We examine the power struggles and ideological differences within the Nazi party, as well as the rise of dissenting voices who sought to overthrow Hitler's regime.

Through a historical lens, this subchapter sheds light on the intricate details of Operation Valkyrie and its impact on Germany, World War II, and subsequent historical events. By analyzing the failed assassination attempt, we gain a deeper understanding of the motivations, mindset, and political climate that shaped this pivotal moment in history.

Consequences and Countermeasures by the Nazis

The failed assassination attempt against Adolf Hitler, known as Operation Valkyrie, had significant consequences and led to a series of countermeasures by the Nazis. This subchapter delves into the aftermath of the plot and its implications for Nazi Germany, the war, and the individuals involved.

Immediately after the failed assassination attempt, Hitler's regime unleashed a wave of brutal retaliation. The conspirators, including key individuals such as Claus von Stauffenberg and Friedrich Olbricht, were swiftly arrested, interrogated, and executed. The Nazi regime sought to eradicate any remnants of dissent within its ranks, purging suspected conspirators and tightening its grip on power.

The consequences of Operation Valkyrie were not limited to the conspirators alone. Hitler's survival bolstered his standing within the Nazi party and the German populace, allowing him to consolidate his power further. The failed assassination attempt also fueled Hitler's paranoia, leading to a climate of fear and suspicion within Nazi Germany.

Furthermore, Operation Valkyrie had a profound impact on the course of World War II. Hitler's survival meant that his aggressive policies and military strategies continued unabated. The failed plot did not deter the Nazis from their path of conquest and genocide. Instead, it solidified their resolve and intensified their efforts to crush resistance movements within Germany and occupied territories.

In response to the attempted assassination, the Nazis implemented stringent security measures to prevent future plots against Hitler's life. The Gestapo, under the leadership of Heinrich Himmler, expanded its surveillance networks, infiltrating resistance groups and tightening control over the German population. The Nazi regime also intensified its propaganda campaign, depicting the conspirators as traitors and enemies of the state.

The failed assassination attempt and its aftermath had a profound impact on the German resistance movements. While Operation Valkyrie did not achieve its immediate objective of removing Hitler from power, it galvanized opposition forces and inspired further acts of resistance. The failed plot became a symbol of defiance against the Nazi regime, encouraging others to join the fight against Hitler's tyranny.

Operation Valkyrie and its consequences also reverberated beyond Nazi Germany. The failed assassination plot captured the attention of the world and became a case study in political assassinations. Historians and conspiracy theorists have extensively analyzed the intricacies of the plot, examining the motivations, strategies, and failures of the conspirators.

Moreover, the story of Operation Valkyrie has had a lasting cultural influence. It has been depicted in literature, film, and other forms of popular culture, cementing its place in the collective memory. The psychological profiles of the conspirators have been dissected, shedding light on the motivations and mindset of those who risked their lives to oppose Hitler's regime.

In conclusion, the consequences and countermeasures by the Nazis in response to Operation Valkyrie were far-reaching. The failed assassination attempt had significant repercussions for Nazi Germany, the war, and the individuals involved. It intensified Hitler's grip on power, fueled his paranoia, and led to brutal reprisals against the conspirators. However, it also inspired further resistance and became a symbol of defiance against the Nazi regime. The story of Operation Valkyrie continues to captivate historians, conspiracy theorists, and those interested in understanding the complexities of World War II and political assassinations.

Chapter 5: German Resistance Movements: Opposing Hitler's Regime

The Kreisau Circle: A Hub of Anti-Nazi Resistance

In the dark shadows of Nazi Germany, a secret group of individuals emerged, united by their shared belief in the need to overthrow Adolf Hitler's tyrannical regime. This subchapter explores the remarkable story of the Kreisau Circle, a hub of anti-Nazi resistance that played a pivotal role in Operation Valkyrie, the failed assassination attempt against Hitler.

The Kreisau Circle, named after the small Silesian village where they first met, was a diverse group of intellectuals, military officers, and politicians who came together to discuss and plan resistance against the Nazi regime. Led by Helmuth James von Moltke, a young lawyer with a strong moral compass, the circle became a beacon of hope in a country consumed by fear.

The members of the Kreisau Circle recognized the danger posed by Hitler's unchecked power and sought to restore democracy and human rights in Germany. They believed in the values of individual freedom, social justice, and religious tolerance, principles that stood in stark contrast to the Nazi ideology.

Through their intellectual discussions and clandestine meetings, the members of the Kreisau Circle developed a comprehensive vision for a post-Hitler Germany. They explored strategies for political resistance, military tactics, and plans for a new constitutional framework that would safeguard democracy.

The circle's influence extended beyond its immediate members. It acted as a catalyst, inspiring other resistance groups and individuals to join the fight against Hitler's tyranny. Their message of hope and resistance spread like wildfire, igniting a spark of defiance in the hearts of those who yearned for freedom.

Tragically, Operation Valkyrie, the culmination of the Kreisau Circle's efforts, failed. Hitler survived the assassination attempt, and the repercussions were devastating. Many members of the Kreisau Circle were arrested, tortured, and executed, paying the ultimate price for their beliefs.

Yet, their legacy lives on. The Kreisau Circle remains a symbol of courage, resilience, and unwavering commitment to principles in the face of overwhelming odds. Their story serves as a reminder that even in the darkest of times, there are those who refuse to surrender to tyranny.

For historians, the tale of the Kreisau Circle offers a wealth of insights into the complexities of resistance movements, the power of ideas, and the human spirit's indomitable nature. It provides a unique lens through which to explore Operation Valkyrie, World War II conspiracies, German resistance movements, and the internal conflicts within Nazi Germany.

By delving into the motivations and mindset of the conspirators, historians can gain a deeper understanding of the psychological profiles of those involved in the assassination plot against Hitler. Moreover, the impacts of Operation Valkyrie, both in terms of Hitler's rule and the course of the war, offer a fascinating avenue for analysis.

Finally, the cultural influence of Operation Valkyrie cannot be underestimated. The story of the Kreisau Circle has captivated audiences across the globe, inspiring numerous works of literature, film, and other forms of popular culture. Its enduring legacy is a testament to the power of storytelling and the importance of remembering the brave individuals who risked everything for the sake of freedom.

The White Rose Movement: Student Activism Against Hitler

During World War II, a group of university students in Munich, Germany, took a courageous stand against Adolf Hitler and his Nazi regime. Known as the White Rose Movement, these young individuals risked their lives to distribute anti-Nazi pamphlets and raise awareness about the atrocities being committed by the German government. Their story is a testament to the power of student activism and the unwavering commitment to justice.

The White Rose Movement was founded in 1942 by Hans Scholl, a medical student, and his sister Sophie Scholl, a philosophy student. They were joined by Alexander Schmorell, Willi Graf, Christoph Probst, and other like-minded individuals who believed in the principles of freedom, justice, and human rights. Together, they formed a clandestine resistance group that aimed to awaken the German people to the horrors of Hitler's regime.

The White Rose members used their academic connections to secretly print and distribute six anti-Nazi leaflets. These leaflets contained powerful messages denouncing Hitler, the war, and the persecution of Jews. Their words were a call to action, urging their fellow citizens to resist the Nazi regime and refuse to participate in its crimes.

The White Rose Movement faced immense danger and risked their lives with every pamphlet they distributed. In 1943, the group's activities were discovered by the Gestapo, the Nazi secret police. Hans and Sophie Scholl, along with Christoph Probst, were arrested and ultimately executed for their involvement in the resistance. Despite their tragic fate, their courage and conviction inspired others to continue fighting against Hitler's tyrannical rule.

The White Rose Movement remains a symbol of resistance and defiance against oppression. Their story has been celebrated in literature, film, and other forms of popular culture, ensuring that their message continues to resonate with future generations. Additionally, their actions shed light on the existence of internal conflicts within Nazi Germany, as many individuals, including students, rejected Hitler's ideology and sought to bring about change.

The impact of the White Rose Movement and their defiance against Hitler cannot be underestimated. They demonstrated that even in the face of overwhelming power and persecution, a small group of dedicated individuals can make a difference. Their bravery serves as a reminder that the fight for justice and freedom is an ongoing struggle that requires the unwavering commitment of all individuals.

In conclusion, the White Rose Movement stands as a testament to the power of student activism and the resilience of the human spirit. Their unwavering commitment to justice and their defiance against Hitler's Nazi regime continues to inspire historians and individuals interested in World War II, German resistance movements, and political assassinations. Their story serves as a reminder of the importance of standing up against oppression, no matter the odds.

Other Resistance Groups and Individuals Within Germany

In addition to the key figures involved in Operation Valkyrie, there were several other resistance groups and individuals within Germany who actively opposed Adolf Hitler's regime during World War II. These lesser-known heroes played crucial roles in the fight against tyranny and deserve recognition for their bravery and sacrifices.

One notable resistance group was the White Rose, composed primarily of students from the University of Munich. Led by siblings Hans and Sophie Scholl, the White Rose distributed anti-Nazi leaflets, calling for passive resistance and the overthrow of Hitler's government. Despite the risks involved, they courageously spoke out against the atrocities committed by the Nazi regime and paid the ultimate price for their actions.

Another prominent figure in the German resistance was Pastor Dietrich Bonhoeffer. As a prominent theologian and staunch opponent of Hitler, Bonhoeffer actively worked within the Confessing Church to resist the Nazi regime. He played a vital role in the German Resistance, providing support to the plotters of Operation Valkyrie and participating in various clandestine activities. Sadly, Bonhoeffer was arrested by the Gestapo and executed in April 1945, mere weeks before the fall of the Third Reich.

The Kreisau Circle, led by Helmuth James Graf von Moltke, was yet another resistance group that operated within Germany. Comprised of intellectuals and aristocrats, the Kreisau Circle aimed to establish a post-Hitler Germany based on democratic principles. They developed plans for a decentralized federal state, emphasizing the importance of individual freedoms and human rights.

Other resistance groups, such as the Red Orchestra and the Edelweiss Pirates, also played vital roles in opposing Hitler's regime. The Red Orchestra, an underground Soviet spy network, gathered intelligence and disseminated anti-Nazi propaganda. The Edelweiss Pirates, on the other hand, were young rebels who engaged in acts of sabotage and distributed anti-war literature.

While Operation Valkyrie is often considered the pinnacle of the German resistance movement, it is crucial to acknowledge the contributions of these other resistance groups and individuals. Their unwavering commitment to justice and freedom in the face of overwhelming odds serves as a testament to the indomitable spirit of the German people during one of the darkest periods in history.

By exploring the stories of these lesser-known resistance groups and individuals, historians can gain a more comprehensive understanding of the complexities and diversity of the German resistance movement. Their actions provide valuable insights into the motivations, strategies, and challenges faced by those who dared to defy Hitler's tyranny.

Chapter 6: Nazi Germany's Internal Conflicts: Power Struggles and the Assassination Attempt

The Rivalry between the Wehrmacht and SS

In the tumultuous landscape of Nazi Germany during World War II, a fierce rivalry emerged between two powerful factions within Hitler's regime: the Wehrmacht and the SS. This subchapter delves into the complexities of this rivalry, shedding light on the tensions, power struggles, and consequences that shaped the course of history.

The Wehrmacht, the regular German army, and the SS, the paramilitary organization responsible for Hitler's security and the implementation of Nazi ideology, represented two distinct power structures within the Third Reich. The Wehrmacht, led by seasoned military officers, prided itself on its long-standing traditions, discipline, and military prowess. On the other hand, the SS, under the command of Heinrich Himmler, embodied the fanaticism and radicalism of the Nazi regime, driven by a ruthless commitment to Hitler's ideology.

The rivalry between these two factions was fueled by overlapping spheres of influence and clashing ambitions. The Wehrmacht resented the SS's encroachment into military matters, seeing it as a threat to their authority and professionalism. Meanwhile, the SS sought to expand its power and influence, challenging the traditional hierarchy of the Wehrmacht.

Operation Valkyrie, the failed assassination attempt against Hitler, became a catalyst for the intensification of this rivalry. Many key individuals involved in the plot were high-ranking officers within the Wehrmacht, who saw the assassination as a necessary step to protect Germany's honor and end the war. They believed that removing Hitler from power would allow them to negotiate a peace treaty with the Allies and salvage what remained of Germany's dignity.

The SS, however, viewed the assassination plot as an act of treason and a threat to their vision of a racially pure and totalitarian state. They quickly moved to suppress the conspirators, further exacerbating the tensions between the two factions.

Ultimately, the rivalry between the Wehrmacht and SS had far-reaching consequences. The failed assassination attempt led to a brutal crackdown on the German resistance movement, resulting in the execution of numerous conspirators. It also solidified the SS's grip on power, as Hitler entrusted them with the task of purging Germany of any dissenting voices.

Understanding the dynamics of this rivalry provides valuable insights into the internal conflicts within Nazi Germany. It highlights the complexities of power dynamics, ideological clashes, and the tragic consequences that unfolded during Operation Valkyrie. By exploring this rivalry, historians can gain a deeper understanding of the motivations, actions, and mindset of the key individuals involved in the assassination plot against Hitler.

Opposition Within the Nazi Party: Conflicting Interests and Motives

The subchapter titled "Opposition Within the Nazi Party: Conflicting Interests and Motives" delves into the intricate web of internal conflicts and power struggles within the Nazi party that ultimately led to the failed assassination attempt against Adolf Hitler in 1944. This subchapter aims to provide historians and enthusiasts with a comprehensive understanding of the various factors that contributed to the formation of the resistance movement within Nazi Germany.

At the heart of the opposition were conflicting interests and motives among key individuals within the Nazi party. While some members of the party recognized the destructive path Hitler was leading Germany towards, others were motivated by personal ambitions or ideological differences. These individuals, often operating in secret, formed alliances and networks to plan and execute the assassination attempt, known as Operation Valkyrie.

One prominent figure within the opposition was Colonel Claus von Stauffenberg, who played a pivotal role in organizing the plot. Stauffenberg, driven by a deep sense of patriotism and disillusionment with Hitler's leadership, sought to overthrow the regime and establish a new government that would save Germany from imminent destruction. Alongside him were other high-ranking military officials, politicians, and intellectuals who shared his vision.

However, the opposition was far from unified. Some members sought to replace Hitler with a military dictatorship, while others advocated for a return to a constitutional monarchy. These conflicting interests created tensions and hindered the effectiveness of the resistance movement. Furthermore, the conspirators faced challenges in gaining widespread support within the Nazi party due to the regime's strict control over information and the extensive Gestapo surveillance.

This subchapter also explores the influence of external factors on the internal conflicts within the Nazi party. The progress of World War II and the deteriorating situation on the Eastern and Western fronts played a significant role in shaping the motivations and actions of the conspirators. As Germany faced increasing setbacks, some party members saw the assassination of Hitler as a last-ditch effort to salvage the country's reputation and potentially negotiate a more favorable peace treaty.

Understanding the conflicting interests and motives within the Nazi party is essential to comprehending the complexity of Operation Valkyrie. By examining the power struggles, ideological differences, and personal ambitions of the individuals involved, historians can gain valuable insights into the dynamics of resistance movements, the challenges they faced, and the impact they had on the course of history.

The Influence of Internal Conflicts on Operation Valkyrie

In the subchapter titled "The Influence of Internal Conflicts on Operation Valkyrie," we delve into the intricate power struggles and internal conflicts within the Nazi party that ultimately led to the failed assassination attempt against Adolf Hitler in 1944. This chapter aims to provide historians and enthusiasts of Operation Valkyrie with a comprehensive understanding of the internal dynamics that influenced the plot and its subsequent consequences.

To fully comprehend the context of Operation Valkyrie, it is crucial to explore the various factions within the Nazi regime that opposed Hitler's leadership and sought to remove him from power. These internal conflicts were fueled by ideological differences, personal rivalries, and disillusionment with Hitler's policies. We analyze the key players involved in the assassination plot, such as Claus von Stauffenberg, Henning von Tresckow, and Ludwig Beck, and their motivations behind joining the resistance movement.

Furthermore, this subchapter delves into the complex relationships between the conspirators and their interactions with other high-ranking officials in the Nazi party. We examine the delicate balance between secrecy and the need to garner support from influential figures who shared their discontent with Hitler's leadership. The internal conflicts within the Nazi party played a crucial role in shaping the plot, as they affected the conspirators' ability to gain the necessary resources and support for their mission.

Additionally, we explore how these internal conflicts impacted the planning and execution of Operation Valkyrie. The conspirators had to navigate a treacherous landscape of mistrust and betrayal, which posed significant challenges to their mission. We analyze how these internal divisions influenced the strategies, tactics, and intelligence networks employed during the plot.

Finally, we examine the consequences of the failed assassination attempt on Hitler's rule and the course of World War II. The internal conflicts within the Nazi party that contributed to Operation Valkyrie had far-reaching implications for the German resistance movements and the future of the war. We assess how these conflicts shaped subsequent events and impacted the broader historical narrative.

This subchapter provides historians and enthusiasts with an in-depth analysis of the internal conflicts that influenced Operation Valkyrie. By understanding the complex dynamics within the Nazi party, readers can gain a deeper appreciation for the motivations, actions, and consequences of the individuals involved in this pivotal moment in history.

Chapter 7: Political Assassinations in History: Operation Valkyrie as a Case Study

Historical Overview of Political Assassinations

Political assassinations have long been a method used by individuals and groups to bring about significant changes in the course of history. From Julius Caesar to John F. Kennedy, these acts of violence have captivated the imaginations of historians and the general public alike. One such assassination attempt that continues to intrigue scholars is Operation Valkyrie, the failed plot to assassinate Adolf Hitler in 1944.

Operation Valkyrie is a fascinating case study in the realm of political assassinations. It not only sheds light on the intricate dynamics of Nazi Germany's internal conflicts but also highlights the bravery and determination of the resistance movements within the country. By examining the key individuals involved in this audacious plot, historians gain valuable insights into the motivations and mindset of those who risked their lives to challenge Hitler's regime.

The failed assassination attempt on Hitler's life had far-reaching consequences, not only for the course of World War II but also for the subsequent global political landscape. By analyzing the military strategy and tactics employed during Operation Valkyrie, historians can gain a deeper understanding of the complexities of the plot and the subsequent military actions that followed.

Moreover, Operation Valkyrie offers a unique opportunity to explore the intelligence networks and secret operations that were in place during World War II. The intricate planning and execution of the assassination attempt reveal the extent to which espionage and covert activities played a role in shaping the course of the war.

The impact of Operation Valkyrie extends beyond the realm of military and political history. The story of this failed assassination attempt has been depicted in various forms of popular culture, including literature, film, and other artistic mediums. By exploring Valkyrie's cultural influence, historians can gain a deeper understanding of how this event continues to resonate with audiences today.

Ultimately, a historical overview of political assassinations, using Operation Valkyrie as a case study, provides historians with a wealth of knowledge and insights. It allows for a comprehensive examination of the motivations behind such acts, the strategies employed, and the consequences that follow. By delving into the lives and backgrounds of the key individuals involved, historians can piece together a more nuanced understanding of political assassinations throughout history, shedding light on their complexities and reverberations.

Similarities and Differences with Operation Valkyrie

Operation Valkyrie, the failed assassination attempt against Adolf Hitler in 1944, remains one of the most captivating events in World War II history. This subchapter aims to explore the similarities and differences between Operation Valkyrie and other significant events and topics that may intrigue historians and enthusiasts alike.

One key similarity lies in the historical biographies of the key individuals involved in the assassination plot. Just as Operation Valkyrie focuses on the lives and backgrounds of the conspirators, there are other historical biographies that shed light on the motivations and actions of key figures in various political assassinations throughout history. By delving into these biographies, historians can draw parallels and analyze the factors that led individuals to take such extreme measures.

Another fascinating aspect to consider is the world of espionage and intelligence during World War II. Operation Valkyrie required a complex network of secret operations and intelligence gathering, much like other covert missions during the war. By examining the intelligence networks involved in planning the assassination attempt, historians can gain a deeper understanding of the strategies employed and the challenges faced by the conspirators.

Furthermore, exploring the impacts of Operation Valkyrie provides an opportunity to delve into the consequences and aftermath of failed political assassinations. This subchapter can analyze how the failed plot influenced Hitler's rule and the course of the war. By examining the broader implications of Operation Valkyrie, historians can gain insights into the potential outcomes of political assassinations and their effects on historical events.

In addition to these similarities, it is crucial to explore the differences between Operation Valkyrie and related topics. For instance, German resistance movements played a significant role in opposing Hitler's regime, and while Operation Valkyrie was a prominent event, it was just one aspect of the broader resistance efforts. By investigating the various resistance groups and individuals within Germany, historians can gain a comprehensive understanding of the internal conflicts and power struggles within Nazi Germany that ultimately led to the assassination attempt.

Lastly, this subchapter can touch upon the cultural influence of Operation Valkyrie. Exploring how the story has been depicted in literature, film, and popular culture offers a unique perspective on the enduring impact of the failed plot. By examining the various forms of media that have portrayed Operation Valkyrie, historians can analyze the ways in which historical events are interpreted and remembered.

In conclusion, this subchapter aims to highlight the similarities and differences between Operation Valkyrie and various related topics, including historical biographies, World War II conspiracies, military strategy, German resistance movements, Nazi Germany's internal conflicts, political assassinations, intelligence and espionage, the impacts of the operation, Valkyrie's cultural influence, and the psychological profiles of the conspirators. By exploring these connections, historians can gain a deeper understanding of Operation Valkyrie and its significance within the broader context of history.

Lessons Learned from Failed Assassination Attempts

Assassination attempts have always captured the imagination of historians and conspiracy theorists alike. The failed assassination attempt against Adolf Hitler, famously known as Operation Valkyrie, is one such event that continues to intrigue and captivate audiences worldwide. In this subchapter, we delve into the lessons learned from this audacious plot, which aimed to rid the world of one of history's most notorious figures.

The key individuals involved in Operation Valkyrie possessed unwavering determination and a fervent belief in their cause. However, their failure offers invaluable insights into the complexities of political assassinations and the challenges they entail. By examining the mistakes made during this operation, historians can gain a deeper understanding of the intricate nature of such plots.

One crucial lesson that emerges from Operation Valkyrie is the importance of thorough planning and meticulous execution. The conspirators' failure to eliminate Hitler can be attributed, in part, to their inability to coordinate their efforts effectively. This highlights the significance of clear communication channels, well-defined roles, and a comprehensive strategy when attempting to overthrow a regime or assassinate a leader.

Another lesson learned from this failed attempt is the need for a diverse and well-connected network of individuals. Operation Valkyrie demonstrated the limitations of relying on a small group of conspirators. In order to achieve success, future plots should involve a broader network of individuals with different skills, backgrounds, and connections. This would enhance their chances of gathering intelligence, acquiring resources, and effectively executing their plan.

Furthermore, Operation Valkyrie highlights the importance of understanding the psychological profiles of the conspirators. By delving into their motivations and mindset, historians can uncover the factors that influenced their decision-making process. This knowledge can help in identifying potential weaknesses and vulnerabilities within the group, ultimately leading to a more effective and successful plot.

Lastly, the failed assassination attempt against Hitler underscores the need for adaptability and flexibility. As circumstances change, so too must the plans and strategies employed by the conspirators. Operation Valkyrie's rigidity and inability to adapt to evolving conditions ultimately sealed its fate. Future plots must be dynamic and responsive, capable of adjusting to unforeseen challenges and seizing new opportunities as they arise.

In conclusion, the failed assassination attempt against Adolf Hitler in Operation Valkyrie offers valuable lessons for historians, conspiracy theorists, and anyone interested in the intricacies of political assassinations. Thorough planning, coordination, a diverse network, understanding psychological profiles, and adaptability are key takeaways from this historic event. By learning from the mistakes made in Operation Valkyrie, future plots can strive for greater success in their mission to challenge oppressive regimes and reshape history.

Chapter 8: Intelligence and Espionage during World War II: Planning the Assassination Attempt

Secret Networks and Covert Operations

In the subchapter "Secret Networks and Covert Operations," we delve into the clandestine world of Operation Valkyrie and the intricate web of secret networks and covert operations that were involved in the failed assassination attempt against Adolf Hitler in 1944. This chapter sheds light on the hidden aspects of one of the most audacious plots in history and explores its implications on various niches, including military strategy, historical biographies, and World War II conspiracies.

At the heart of Operation Valkyrie were a group of key individuals who risked their lives to challenge Hitler's regime. These individuals formed secret networks, establishing covert communication channels, safe houses, and intelligence gathering operations. Through their efforts, they aimed to undermine the Nazi regime from within and restore democracy to Germany.

The chapter examines the motivation and mindset of the conspirators, providing psychological profiles that offer insights into their determination and bravery. It explores their backgrounds, shedding light on their personal experiences and the events that led them to take such extreme measures. By analyzing their stories, we gain a deeper understanding of the individuals behind the assassination attempt and the sacrifices they made for their beliefs.

Furthermore, the chapter delves into the intelligence and espionage networks involved in planning Operation Valkyrie. It uncovers the intricate web of spies, double agents, and informants who risked their lives to gather crucial information and aid the conspirators in their mission. These secret operations played a vital role in the plot's planning and execution.

The subchapter also explores the consequences and aftermath of the failed assassination attempt. It examines the impact on Hitler's rule and the course of the war, as well as the internal conflicts within the Nazi party that led to the assassination attempt. By examining the power struggles and conflicts within the party, we gain insight into the broader dynamics of Nazi Germany during this critical period.

Finally, "Secret Networks and Covert Operations" delves into Operation Valkyrie's cultural influence. It explores how the story has been depicted in literature, film, and popular culture, highlighting its enduring significance and the lessons it offers for humanity.

Overall, this subchapter provides historians with a comprehensive analysis of the secret networks and covert operations that shaped Operation Valkyrie. It is an essential read for those interested in military strategy, historical biographies, World War II conspiracies, German resistance movements, and the broader implications of political assassinations throughout history.

Infiltration of the German Military and Government

The infiltration of the German military and government played a pivotal role in the planning and execution of Operation Valkyrie, the failed assassination attempt against Adolf Hitler in 1944. This subchapter delves into the intricate details of how key individuals managed to infiltrate the highest echelons of power, highlighting their motivations, methods, and the consequences of their actions.

In the midst of World War II, a group of German military officers and government officials, disillusioned with Hitler's leadership and the atrocities committed by the Nazi regime, conspired to eliminate the dictator and restore Germany's honor. To achieve their goal, these individuals had to clandestinely infiltrate the very institutions they sought to overthrow.

Operating within the German military and government, the conspirators skillfully disguised their intentions, ensuring their involvement remained hidden from Hitler's loyalists. They strategically positioned themselves in influential positions, allowing them access to classified information and the ability to influence decision-making processes.

The infiltration efforts required careful maneuvering and delicate balancing acts. The conspirators needed to maintain the appearance of loyalty to the regime, all while secretly working towards Hitler's downfall. Their success relied on their ability to operate in the shadows, leveraging their positions to gather intelligence, recruit like-minded individuals, and plan their assassination plot.

The consequences of their infiltration were far-reaching. As the conspirators gained access to classified information, they were able to gather crucial intelligence on Hitler's military strategies, enabling them to plan their assassination attempt with precision. Additionally, their presence within the German military and government provided a platform for spreading dissent, inspiring other individuals to question Hitler's regime and potentially join the resistance movement.

However, the risks of infiltration were immense. Discovery would have resulted in swift and brutal consequences, not only for the infiltrators themselves but also for their families and associates. The conspirators were acutely aware of the dangers they faced, but their commitment to restoring Germany's honor and ending the war motivated them to take these risks.

The infiltration of the German military and government during Operation Valkyrie stands as a testament to the bravery, cunning, and determination of these key individuals. Their actions not only shed light on the internal conflicts within Nazi Germany but also provide valuable insights into the broader themes of political assassinations, resistance movements, military strategy, and espionage during World War II.

By examining the motivations and mindset of the conspirators, historians can gain a deeper understanding of the complex factors that drove individuals to take such audacious actions. The infiltration efforts and subsequent assassination attempt against Hitler had a profound impact on the course of the war and the subsequent historical narrative. As such, it is crucial to explore their story within the context of Operation Valkyrie, as well as its broader implications for Nazi Germany and the world.

Gathering Intelligence for Operation Valkyrie

In the subchapter "Gathering Intelligence for Operation Valkyrie," we delve into the intricate web of intelligence networks and secret operations that played a crucial role in planning the failed assassination attempt against Adolf Hitler in 1944. This chapter aims to provide historians and enthusiasts of Operation Valkyrie with a detailed understanding of the intelligence-gathering process and its significance in the wider context of World War II.

To comprehend the complexities of Operation Valkyrie, it is essential to examine the various sources and methods used to gather intelligence. We explore the role of undercover agents, resistance groups, and individuals within Germany who opposed Hitler's regime. From high-ranking military officials to disillusioned Nazi sympathizers, the conspirators relied on a vast network of informants to gather critical information about Hitler's movements, his security measures, and the inner workings of the Nazi party.

Furthermore, this chapter delves into the challenges faced by the intelligence operatives. We explore the risks they took, often at the cost of their own lives, to collect and transmit information. From encrypted messages to secret meetings, the conspirators had to navigate a treacherous landscape of surveillance and suspicion, all while ensuring the utmost secrecy to avoid detection by the Gestapo.

In addition to the gathering of intelligence, we examine the analysis and decision-making process behind Operation Valkyrie. Military strategy and tactics are analyzed in detail, exploring the strengths and weaknesses of the assassination plot. We delve into the meticulous planning, the intricate timing, and the calculated risks taken by the conspirators.

By understanding the intelligence operations and military strategy behind Operation Valkyrie, historians gain a deeper insight into the motivations and mindset of the individuals involved. Psychological profiles of the conspirators are explored, shedding light on their motivations, fears, and personal sacrifices.

This subchapter not only provides a comprehensive account of the intelligence and espionage networks involved in Operation Valkyrie but also sheds light on the broader implications of the failed assassination attempt. The consequences and aftermath of the plot are examined, including the impact on Hitler's rule and the course of the war.

Operation Valkyrie continues to captivate historians, as well as those interested in World War II conspiracies, military strategy, and political assassinations in history. It has also made a significant impact on popular culture, with its depiction in literature, film, and other forms of media. By exploring the intelligence operations and psychological profiles of the conspirators, this subchapter aims to deepen our understanding of this pivotal event in history.

Chapter 9: Impacts of Operation Valkyrie: Consequences and Aftermath

Hitler's Response: Retribution and Crackdown on the Resistance

After narrowly escaping death in the failed assassination attempt known as Operation Valkyrie, Adolf Hitler unleashed a wave of retribution and crackdown on the resistance movements within Germany. Hitler's response was swift, brutal, and calculated, as he sought to eliminate any trace of dissent and solidify his power.

Hitler, enraged by the audacity of the conspirators, ordered a ruthless crackdown on the resistance groups that had been operating in the shadows. The Gestapo, under Heinrich Himmler's command, intensified their efforts to dismantle these underground networks. Thousands were arrested, tortured, and executed, with no mercy shown to those suspected of involvement in the plot.

In addition to the brutal crackdown, Hitler also sought to tighten his grip on power and eliminate any potential threats within his own party. The failed assassination attempt had exposed a deep divide within the Nazi ranks, with some high-ranking officials secretly sympathizing with the conspirators. Hitler purged the party of suspected traitors, carrying out a series of arrests and executions.

The failed assassination attempt also had significant implications for Germany's military strategy and tactics during World War II. Hitler, already paranoid and suspicious of his generals, became even more erratic and unpredictable. He began to micromanage military operations, distrusting his officers and implementing risky strategies that ultimately led to disastrous defeats for the German forces.

The impact of Operation Valkyrie extended beyond the immediate aftermath of the failed plot. It had far-reaching consequences for Hitler's rule and the course of the war. The failed assassination attempt served as a rallying point for the German people, strengthening their support for Hitler and the Nazi regime. It also solidified Hitler's resolve to crush any dissent and reinforced his belief in his own invincibility.

Operation Valkyrie has since become a significant case study in the broader exploration of political assassinations throughout history. Historians have examined the motivations and mindset of the individuals involved, delving into the psychological profiles of the conspirators to better understand their actions. The story of Operation Valkyrie has also been depicted in literature, film, and other forms of popular culture, highlighting its cultural influence and enduring fascination.

In conclusion, Hitler's response to the failed assassination attempt was one of retribution and crackdown on the resistance movements within Germany. The brutal and calculated measures taken by Hitler and his loyalists aimed to eliminate any trace of dissent and solidify his power. The failed plot had far-reaching consequences for Germany's military strategy, internal conflicts within the Nazi party, and the course of the war. Operation Valkyrie continues to captivate historians, conspiracy theorists, and those interested in the complexities of World War II and political assassinations.

The Course of World War II: How Operation Valkyrie Shaped History

Operation Valkyrie is a significant event in World War II that continues to captivate historians and enthusiasts alike. This subchapter delves into the multifaceted impact of the failed assassination attempt against Adolf Hitler on July 20, 1944, focusing on how it shaped the course of the war and influenced subsequent historical narratives.

Examining the historical biographies of the key individuals involved provides a deeper understanding of the motivations and backgrounds of the conspirators. From high-ranking military officers like Claus von Stauffenberg to lesser-known figures, their stories shed light on the complex web of resistance against Hitler's regime.

Operation Valkyrie also gives rise to numerous conspiracy theories, prompting discussions about Hitler's survival and the extent of Nazi infiltration. Exploring these theories within the context of the failed assassination plot allows historians to analyze the various perspectives and evaluate their plausibility.

Military strategy and tactics played a crucial role in Operation Valkyrie. Analyzing the intricacies of the plot and the subsequent actions during the war provides valuable insights into the challenges faced by the resistance movement and the impact of their actions on the larger conflict.

The German resistance movements and individuals who opposed Hitler's regime offer a fascinating area of study. Investigating their motivations, strategies, and the risks they undertook helps to paint a comprehensive picture of the internal conflicts within Nazi Germany.

The power struggles and internal conflicts within the Nazi party that led to the assassination attempt are also worth exploring. Understanding the dynamics within the party sheds light on the potential vulnerabilities that contributed to the plot's conception and execution.

Operation Valkyrie serves as a case study for broader exploration into political assassinations throughout history. By examining the historical context, motivations, and consequences of the plot, historians can draw parallels and gain a deeper understanding of the impact of such events on the course of history.

Intelligence and espionage played a crucial role in planning Operation Valkyrie. Focusing on the intelligence networks and secret operations involved in the plot provides insights into the level of organization and coordination required for such a daring operation.

The failed assassination attempt had far-reaching consequences that impacted Hitler's rule and the course of the war. Examining the aftermath of Operation Valkyrie allows historians to evaluate its role as a turning point in the conflict and the subsequent actions taken by the Nazi regime.

Operation Valkyrie's cultural influence is also worth exploring. From literature to film and other forms of popular culture, its depiction has shaped public perception and understanding of the plot. Analyzing these cultural representations provides insights into the broader significance and lasting impact of Operation Valkyrie.

Lastly, delving into the psychological profiles of the conspirators offers a unique perspective on their motivations and mindset. Understanding the psychological factors that influenced their decisions helps to humanize these individuals and provides a richer understanding of their actions.

In conclusion, Operation Valkyrie is a pivotal event in World War II that holds immense historical significance. By exploring its impact on various aspects of history, from military strategy to political assassinations and cultural influence, historians can gain a comprehensive understanding of how this failed assassination attempt shaped the course of the war and continues to shape our understanding of history.

Legacy and Historical Significance of the Failed Assassination Attempt

The failed assassination attempt against Adolf Hitler in 1944, known as Operation Valkyrie, holds immense historical significance and continues to captivate the attention of historians and enthusiasts alike. This subchapter aims to delve into the lasting legacy and historical impact left by this audacious plot.

Operation Valkyrie serves as a gateway to explore a multitude of niches within historical research. For those interested in World War II conspiracies, it offers a fascinating glimpse into the various conspiracy theories surrounding Hitler's survival and the potential alternate outcomes if the plot had succeeded.

From a military strategy and tactics perspective, the intricate details of the assassination plot and the subsequent military actions during the war provide a wealth of analysis. Historians can delve into the strategic planning, communication networks, and logistical challenges faced by the conspirators.

Examining the German resistance movements also becomes essential when exploring Operation Valkyrie. The plot involved a network of brave individuals who opposed Hitler's regime, shedding light on the internal conflicts and power struggles within Nazi Germany. This subchapter offers historians valuable insights into the dynamics of resistance groups and the individuals who risked their lives to challenge Hitler's rule.

Moreover, Operation Valkyrie serves as a case study for political assassinations throughout history. By studying this failed attempt, historians can gain a broader understanding of the motivations, methods, and outcomes of political assassinations in different historical contexts.

Intelligence and espionage during World War II are also central themes within Operation Valkyrie. The planning and execution of the plot necessitated the involvement of various intelligence networks and secret operations. Historians can explore the intricacies of these covert activities, shedding light on the complex world of espionage during the war.

The impacts of Operation Valkyrie cannot be underestimated. Historians can analyze the consequences and aftermath of the failed assassination attempt on Hitler's rule and the course of the war. This subchapter examines the ripple effects on the German government, the morale of the German people, and the broader geopolitical landscape of World War II.

Furthermore, Operation Valkyrie's cultural influence is explored, specifically how the story has been depicted in literature, film, and popular culture. By examining these adaptations, historians can gain insights into the evolving interpretation and perception of this historical event.

Lastly, this subchapter delves into the psychological profiles of the conspirators, providing a unique opportunity to understand the motivations, mindset, and personal experiences of individuals involved in the assassination plot against Hitler. This psychological exploration adds another layer of understanding to the historical context.

In conclusion, the failed assassination attempt against Adolf Hitler in 1944, Operation Valkyrie, has left a lasting legacy and continues to intrigue historians. This subchapter offers a comprehensive exploration of the historical significance of this event, addressing various niches within historical research and providing valuable insights into World War II, resistance movements, conspiracy theories, military strategy, political assassinations, intelligence operations, and cultural influence.

Chapter 10: Valkyrie's Cultural Influence: Depictions in Literature, Film, and Popular Culture

Operation Valkyrie in Books and Novels

Operation Valkyrie, the failed assassination attempt against Adolf Hitler in 1944, has captivated historians, conspiracy theorists, and enthusiasts of World War II for decades. The event itself and the key individuals involved have been extensively explored in numerous books and novels, shedding light on the complexities of the plot, the motivations of the conspirators, and the impact it had on Nazi Germany and the course of the war.

Historical biographies have played a significant role in documenting the lives and backgrounds of the key individuals involved in the assassination attempt. These biographies provide a comprehensive understanding of the personalities and ideologies that influenced their decision to plot against Hitler. By delving into their personal histories, readers gain insight into the internal conflicts within Nazi Germany and the resistance movements that sought to overthrow Hitler's regime.

World War II conspiracies have also been widely explored in relation to Operation Valkyrie. These books and novels delve into various conspiracy theories surrounding the failed assassination attempt and Hitler's alleged survival. They examine the possibility of a wider network of resistance groups and the potential involvement of foreign intelligence agencies. By examining these theories, historians can assess the validity of different claims and gain a deeper understanding of the complexities surrounding this historical event.

Military strategy and tactics are another facet of Operation Valkyrie that has been extensively analyzed in literature. Books and novels that focus on this aspect of the plot provide a detailed examination of the intricacies of the failed assassination attempt and the subsequent military actions during the war. By studying the planning and execution of Operation Valkyrie, military strategists can gain valuable insights into the challenges faced by the conspirators and the impact their actions had on the broader war effort.

German resistance movements and the internal conflicts within Nazi Germany have also been thoroughly investigated in relation to Operation Valkyrie. These books and novels explore the power struggles within the Nazi party that led to the assassination attempt and highlight the individuals and groups who opposed Hitler's regime. By examining these resistance movements, historians can gain a deeper understanding of the complex dynamics within Nazi Germany and the motivations behind the plot to assassinate Hitler.

In addition to the historical aspects, Operation Valkyrie has also had a significant cultural influence. Books, novels, and films have depicted the story of Operation Valkyrie, bringing the events to a wider audience. These works of popular culture explore the motivations and mindset of the conspirators, shedding light on the psychological profiles of the individuals involved. By delving into their motivations, these works provide a deeper understanding of the human element behind the failed assassination attempt.

In conclusion, Operation Valkyrie has been extensively explored in books and novels, appealing to historians and various niches such as historical biographies, World War II conspiracies, military strategy and tactics, German resistance movements, Nazi Germany's internal conflicts, political assassinations, intelligence and espionage during World War II, impacts of Operation Valkyrie, and the cultural influence of Valkyrie. These works provide valuable insights into the key individuals involved, the intricacies of the plot, and the broader historical context in which the failed assassination attempt took place.

Film Adaptations and Portrayals of the Assassination Attempt

The failed assassination attempt against Adolf Hitler in 1944, known as Operation Valkyrie, has captured the imaginations of historians, conspiracy theorists, and filmmakers alike. The dramatic events surrounding the plot to eliminate Hitler and overthrow the Nazi regime have been a source of fascination and inspiration for numerous film adaptations.

One of the most prominent portrayals of Operation Valkyrie came in the form of the 2008 film "Valkyrie," directed by Bryan Singer and starring Tom Cruise as Colonel Claus von Stauffenberg, the key figure in the assassination plot. The film provides a gripping account of the conspirators' efforts to kill Hitler and seize control of Germany. It explores the intricate planning and daring actions of the resistance members, shedding light on the risks they faced and the challenges they encountered.

"Valkyrie" offers a compelling portrayal of the psychological profiles of the conspirators, delving into their motivations and mindset. It highlights their unwavering commitment to their cause and their belief in the necessity of removing Hitler from power. The film also examines the power struggles and internal conflicts within the Nazi party that led to the assassination attempt, shedding light on the complex dynamics that shaped the conspiracy.

In addition to "Valkyrie," there have been other film adaptations that have explored the story of Operation Valkyrie. These include the 1955 German film "Der 20. Juli," directed by Falk Harnack, and the 1994 television movie "Stauffenberg," directed by Jo Baier. Each of these adaptations offers its own unique perspective on the events leading up to the failed assassination attempt, providing further insights into the motivations and actions of the conspirators.

The film adaptations of Operation Valkyrie have not only entertained audiences but have also played a significant role in shaping public perception of the assassination plot. They have brought the story to a wider audience, sparking interest in the historical context and the individuals involved. These films have helped to shed light on the courage and determination of the resistance members and have stimulated further research and exploration of the events surrounding Operation Valkyrie.

In conclusion, the film adaptations of Operation Valkyrie have provided valuable insights into the failed assassination attempt against Adolf Hitler. They have explored the motivations and mindsets of the conspirators, examined the power struggles within the Nazi party, and brought the story to a wider audience. These adaptations have played a significant role in preserving the memory of the individuals involved in the plot and ensuring that their bravery and sacrifice are not forgotten.

Popular Culture References and Perceptions of Operation Valkyrie

Operation Valkyrie, the failed assassination attempt against Adolf Hitler in 1944, has become a significant event in history, capturing the fascination of various audiences and inspiring a range of interpretations in popular culture. From books and films to documentaries and artworks, Operation Valkyrie has left a lasting impact on the collective consciousness, offering historians a unique lens through which to analyze the complexities of the event and its aftermath.

In literature and film, Operation Valkyrie has been portrayed as a tale of heroism and bravery against insurmountable odds. The key individuals involved, such as Claus von Stauffenberg and his co-conspirators, have been depicted as both tragic figures and symbols of resistance against

Hitler's tyrannical regime. These narratives often focus on the personal backgrounds and motivations of the conspirators, delving into their psychological profiles and exploring the moral dilemmas they faced.

Operation Valkyrie has also become a case study in the broader exploration of political assassinations throughout history. Historians have used this event to analyze the power struggles and internal conflicts within the Nazi party that led to the assassination attempt. By studying the intelligence networks and secret operations involved in planning the event, researchers have gained insight into the world of espionage and covert operations during World War II.

Moreover, the cultural influence of Operation Valkyrie cannot be underestimated. Its story has been depicted in various forms of popular culture, including novels, movies, and even video games. These adaptations have not only brought the event to a wider audience but have also sparked debates about the accuracy of their portrayals. The enduring fascination with Operation Valkyrie highlights the enduring grip of World War II on popular culture and the continued interest in exploring the complexities of the era.

For historians, Operation Valkyrie offers a rich tapestry of historical biographies, World War II conspiracies, military strategy and tactics, German resistance movements, Nazi Germany's internal conflicts, political assassinations, intelligence and espionage, and the impacts and aftermath of the failed assassination attempt. By delving into these various aspects, historians can uncover new perspectives and shed light on the significance of Operation Valkyrie within the broader historical context.

Chapter 11: Psychological Profiles of the Conspirators: Motivations and Mindsets

Understanding the Mind of Claus von Stauffenberg

Claus von Stauffenberg, a key figure in the failed assassination attempt against Adolf Hitler known as Operation Valkyrie, remains a fascinating enigma in the annals of history. To truly comprehend the motivations and mindset of this influential individual, it is essential to explore the complex factors that shaped his character and led him to take such a daring and perilous action.

Born into a noble German family in 1907, Stauffenberg grew up amidst a tumultuous period in German history. Witnessing the rise of Adolf Hitler and the Nazi party, Stauffenberg became increasingly disillusioned with the regime's ideology and its devastating impact on the German people. His strong sense of duty, coupled with his deep patriotic convictions, ultimately compelled him to join the resistance movement.

Stauffenberg's military background played a crucial role in shaping his strategic thinking and decision-making process. As an officer in the German army, he possessed a deep understanding of military tactics and the inner workings of the Nazi regime. This knowledge proved invaluable in formulating the audacious plan to assassinate Hitler and seize control of the German government.

However, it is essential to delve beyond Stauffenberg's military acumen to truly understand his mindset. Deeply influenced by his Catholic faith and moral principles, Stauffenberg's motivation was not solely rooted in political opposition to Hitler. He believed that eliminating Hitler was a moral imperative, a necessary act to save Germany and prevent further atrocities.

Stauffenberg's unwavering determination and unwavering belief in the cause of the resistance movement were evident in his unwavering commitment to Operation Valkyrie. Despite the risks and personal sacrifices, he remained resolute in his goal, convinced that his actions could alter the course of history.

To truly comprehend the mind of Claus von Stauffenberg, one must examine the various factors that shaped his character, including his noble upbringing, military background, religious convictions, and unwavering commitment to his cause. By doing so, we gain valuable insights into the motivations and mindset of this remarkable individual, shedding light on the complexities of Operation Valkyrie and its impact on World War II history.

For historians, Operation Valkyrie represents a captivating case study in military strategy, political assassinations, and the psychology of resistance movements. By understanding the mind of Claus von Stauffenberg, we gain a deeper appreciation for the intricate dynamics that drove this key individual, ultimately shaping the course of history.

Henning von Tresckow: Ideals and Determination

Henning von Tresckow, a key figure in Operation Valkyrie, was a man of unwavering ideals and determined resolve. Born into a noble family in Germany in 1901, Tresckow grew up witnessing the rise of Adolf Hitler and the Nazi regime. As a military officer, he was deeply troubled by the atrocities committed by the Nazis and the destruction they were bringing upon his beloved country.

Tresckow's ideals were rooted in a deep sense of duty and honor. He believed in the importance of preserving the values and integrity of the German nation, even if it meant sacrificing his own life. Inspired by his own moral compass, he became a central figure in the resistance movement against Hitler's regime.

Driven by his determination to overthrow Hitler, Tresckow played a crucial role in the planning and execution of Operation Valkyrie, the audacious plot to assassinate the Führer. He meticulously devised strategies, recruited fellow conspirators, and coordinated intelligence networks, all while operating under the constant threat of discovery by the Gestapo.

Tresckow's determination was unmatched, as he recognized the risks involved in his mission but remained undeterred. He firmly believed that the assassination of Hitler was not only necessary to save Germany from further destruction but also to demonstrate to the world that there were Germans who opposed Hitler and his brutal regime.

Despite several failed attempts to assassinate Hitler, Tresckow's determination never wavered. He continued to work tirelessly, constantly adapting his strategies and seeking new opportunities to carry out the plot. His unwavering commitment to his ideals and his determination to see Hitler removed from power made him a pivotal figure in the history of resistance against Nazi Germany.

Henning von Tresckow's ideals and determination serve as an inspiration to historians and enthusiasts interested in Operation Valkyrie and the failed assassination attempt against Hitler. His story sheds light on the bravery and sacrifices made by those who dared to challenge the Nazi regime from within. Tresckow's unwavering commitment to his ideals and his relentless pursuit of justice make him a remarkable historical figure whose legacy continues to resonate to this day.

Examining the Mentalities of Other Key Conspirators

In the subchapter "Examining the Mentalities of Other Key Conspirators," we delve into the intricate world of the individuals involved in Operation Valkyrie, the failed assassination attempt against Adolf Hitler in 1944. This subchapter aims to shed light on the motivations, mindsets, and psychological profiles of the lesser-known conspirators who played crucial roles in the plot.

While Colonel Claus von Stauffenberg's name is synonymous with the Valkyrie operation, there were several other key individuals whose mentalities and experiences shaped the course of events. This subchapter brings to the forefront their stories, allowing historians and enthusiasts to gain a deeper understanding of the diverse characters behind this audacious plan.

From General Friedrich Olbricht, the mastermind behind Operation Valkyrie, to General Friedrich Fromm, whose wavering loyalty and political ambitions added complexity to the plot, each conspirator possessed a unique set of circumstances and beliefs that propelled them towards their fateful decision. By examining their backgrounds, ideologies, and personal motivations, we gain insight into the broader context of resistance movements within Germany during Nazi rule.

Through meticulous research and analysis, this subchapter explores the internal conflicts within the Nazi party that led to the assassination attempt. It delves into the power struggles, conflicting ideologies, and rivalries that plagued Hitler's regime and ultimately paved the way for Operation Valkyrie.

Furthermore, the subchapter investigates the psychological factors that influenced the conspirators' decision-making processes. It explores the profound impact of fear, disillusionment, and moral duty on their mentalities, highlighting the emotional and psychological toll of living under a totalitarian regime.

By examining these lesser-known figures and their mentalities, historians gain a comprehensive understanding of the broader narrative surrounding Operation Valkyrie. This subchapter not only provides valuable insights into the failed assassination attempt against Hitler but also contributes to the fields of historical biographies, World War II conspiracies, military strategy and tactics, German resistance movements, Nazi Germany's internal conflicts, political assassinations in history, intelligence and espionage during World War II, and the impacts and cultural influence of Operation Valkyrie.

Through a multidisciplinary approach, this subchapter enhances our understanding of Operation Valkyrie, shedding light on the intricate web of motivations, mentalities, and personalities that shaped this pivotal moment in history.

Conclusion: Operation Valkyrie's Impact on History and the Study of Political Assassinations

Operation Valkyrie, the failed assassination attempt against Adolf Hitler in 1944, has had a profound impact on history and the study of political assassinations. This event, which involved a group of courageous individuals within the German resistance, has captivated historians and enthusiasts alike, shedding light on various aspects of World War II and the inner workings of Nazi Germany.

First and foremost, Operation Valkyrie has provided historians with invaluable insights into the lives and backgrounds of the key individuals involved in the assassination plot against Hitler. Through meticulous research and analysis, biographers have unravelled the motivations, fears, and ideologies of figures such as Claus von Stauffenberg, Wilhelm Canaris, and others. These historical biographies have not only deepened our understanding of the individuals themselves but have also shed light on the broader scope of resistance movements within Germany during that time.

The failed assassination attempt has also fueled countless conspiracy theories, adding an intriguing layer to the study of Operation Valkyrie. Some theorists speculate on Hitler's survival and the possible involvement of external powers, while others delve into the intricate military strategy and tactics employed during the plot. These discussions have opened avenues for further exploration and debate, expanding our knowledge of World War II conspiracies and the complexities of the era.

Moreover, Operation Valkyrie has highlighted the power struggles and internal conflicts within the Nazi party that ultimately led to the assassination attempt. By examining the different factions and individuals involved, historians have gained valuable insights into the dynamics of Nazi Germany and the factors that contributed to Hitler's regime being challenged from within.

Additionally, the failed assassination attempt has provided a case study for the broader exploration of political assassinations throughout history. Operation Valkyrie serves as a lens through which historians can analyze the motivations, methods, and consequences of political assassinations in various contexts. This comparative analysis enables a deeper understanding of the impact and implications of such events on societies and political systems.

Furthermore, the intelligence networks and secret operations involved in planning Operation Valkyrie have shed light on the intricate world of espionage during World War II. The meticulous planning, coordination, and execution of the plot have captivated military strategists and enthusiasts, offering valuable insights into the challenges faced by intelligence agencies during wartime.

Finally, the consequences and aftermath of Operation Valkyrie have had a lasting impact on Hitler's rule and the course of the war. The failed assassination attempt not only demonstrated the existence of internal opposition within Nazi Germany but also played a significant role in shaping public opinion and international perception of Hitler's regime. The event has been depicted in literature, film, and other forms of popular culture, further cementing its place in history and its cultural influence.

In conclusion, Operation Valkyrie's impact on history and the study of political assassinations cannot be overstated. By examining its various dimensions, including the lives of key individuals, conspiracy theories, military strategy, resistance movements, internal conflicts, intelligence operations, consequences, and cultural influence, historians have gained valuable insights into World War II and the complexities of political assassinations throughout history. Operation Valkyrie stands as a testament to the courage and determination of those who dared to challenge Hitler's regime and has become an enduring symbol of resistance against tyranny.